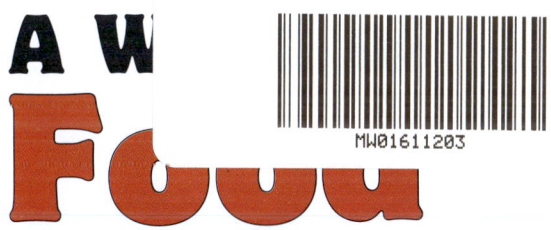

A W
Food

by Franklin Bonaparte

 HOUGHTON MIFFLIN HARCOURT
School Publishers

PHOTOGRAPHY CREDITS: Cover © Peter Casolino/Alamy; 1 © George Glod/SuperStock; 2 © Ed Lallo/Index Stock; 3 © Peter Casolino/Alamy; 4 © Richard Hamilton Smith/Corbis; 5 (l) © David Cook, (m) © Maximilian Stock Ltd, (r) © Getty Images/StockFood; 6 © Frances Roberts/Alamy; 7 © Danny Lehman/Corbis; 8 (l) © Corbis, (r) © George Glod/SuperStock; 9 © Ricardo Azoury/Corbis; 10 (l) © William Gottlieb/Corbis, (m) © Corbis, (r) © Envision/Corbis

What is the first thing you see at the grocery store?
For many people, the answer is fruits and vegetables.
Lots of stores put fruits and vegetables, or produce, at the front.
That's because produce is healthy and delicious.

Grocery stores sell fruits and vegetables.

Your grocery store might sell your favorite fruits.

Your grocery store might sell vegetables that you've never eaten before.

Have you ever wondered where these foods come from?

Let's find out!

Farmers pick produce to sell at a market.

Local Foods

Some produce might be local, or from your area.
Sometimes people like to buy local produce because it is fresh.

pecans   pineapple   avocado

State Foods

Your store might sell produce that your state is famous for.

Georgia is famous for its peaches.

Florida is famous for its oranges.

What kinds of produce grow in your state?

Food from Other Places

Most foods at the store come from far away.

Some fruits and vegetables may not grow well where you live.

So stores get those fruits and vegetables from other places.

Bananas are a good example.
Bananas are this country's most
popular fruit.
But bananas only grow in places
that are very hot and very wet.
So we get our bananas from
Latin America.
The weather there is just right.

Stores also get foods from far away during the winter.

For example, tomatoes only grow in warm weather.

If it is snowing, then the ground is too cold for tomatoes.

So stores get tomatoes from someplace warm.

A farmer picks fruit off a tree.

It takes a lot of work to bring
foods from far away.
People harvest, or pick,
the produce.
Then they pack the produce
in boxes.
Boats, trains, trucks, and airplanes
bring the produce to markets near
and far.

Take a look around your
grocery store.
Notice the different kinds of
produce right under your nose.
Some of it came from nearby.
Some of it came from far away.
You can eat fresh, healthy foods
from around the world all year long!

Responding

Why did the author write this story? What three details about fruits and vegetables tell you this? Make a chart.

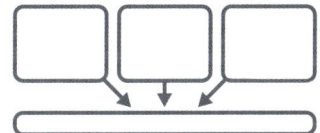

✏️ Talk About It

Text to World Why don't all fruits and vegetables grow in the same place? How do we get fruits and vegetables from faraway places?

WORDS TO KNOW

first	right	under
food	sometimes	your
ground	these	

LEARN MORE WORDS

harvest	market	produce

✔ **TARGET SKILL** **Author's Purpose**
Tell why an author writes a book.

✔ **TARGET STRATEGY** **Summarize** Stop
to tell important ideas as you read.

GENRE **Informational text** gives
facts about a topic.